12 Months From NOW

Book IV (finale)

It's been more like 24…but who's counting

SIR FINIS DeMILO BREWER

12 Months From NOW

12 Months From NOW

Copyright 2015
By SIR FINIS DeMILO BREWER

Published by:
TOOSWEETPUBLISHING productions
P.O.Box 6512 New Orleans, LA. 70174
email: toosweetpublishing.com
website: Toosweetbulishing.com

ISBN: 978-0-941091-05-3

ALL RIGHTS RESERVED. No part of this book can be reproduced electronically, mechanically or by any means without the written permission of the publisher.

First Printing

PRINTED IN THE UNITED STATES OF AMERICA

12 Months From NOW

12 months From Now

Book IV (finale)

Chapter 1 October 26, 2014/Sunday`

"Sometimes…things are not as they seem"

This was the statement being made by the TV evangelist as I walked out the room. I knew it was just one of many messages that the LORD was giving to me after the very long day. The day started at 7:30 a.m. as I got dress for 9:00 service. It was now 3:00pm and I was just getting home from my 3rd church service of the day. And to think the day before, I had no clue as to where the day would begin, let alone end.

I awaken and proceeded to get dress to attend my church "City Church" in the East New Orleans like I normally would do when there is gas in my tank. If I have no money for gas, then I look at the option of catching the bus. But for the past three weeks, my option for busing it has been to just make a way to L.O.C.C. that is in walking distance. By the time I left out of the church on that very first day of attending, I knew GOD had sent me there, and I was now on my latest "Body of Christ" assignment.

So for the past three weeks I'd been attending two churches; my church at 9:00am, and the one the LORD had recently assigned to me. The day he did, I was having trouble getting to my church, so I decided to catch the bus. As I waited for the bus that I thought I had beaten to the bus stop, after about 20 minutes I realized that it had beaten me. So with the next bus not coming for a least an hour, and my not having enough for an all day pass (which I was going to need if I wanted to have a way to get back home), I posed a question to the LORD. I said,

"LORD, maybe you have other plans today."

So as I looked around the neighborhood, I was aware that there were two churches just a few feet away from me at the bus stop. So sensing the urging of the Lord, I announced to myself,

"Ok Lord, not my will, but thy will be done."

…and walked over to what I would soon learn was my next assignment: "L.O.C.C. aka Love Outreach Christian Church". Pastored by a husband and wife team; I was already familiar with their ministry pre-Katrina, and they had a good sized congregation then. The Pastor is joined by a strong anointed wife with a prophetess mantel resting upon her. Now ten (10) years since Katrina, they were in a building they were purchasing, with room for hundreds of new members; but the seats were barely occupied. And from experience, somehow I knew why I was being sent here.

(By the time I made this entry November & December had passed; much of it is a blur now. Three of my daughters had made a birthday, along with a grandchild. My baby brother was out of jail and we had a wonderful Thanksgiving Dinner to celebrate. I didn't get my Christmas present of 100 million dollars, but there is still next year. I didn't make it to the Church Christmas play, because I was not financially able; but overall the year ended

without much tragedy in my life
…THANK GOD!

January 1st 2015, Thursday

Today begins the New Year; This time last year I was living in a rented house with my three (3) youngest daughters in my care. I have not seen them in nine (9) months, and have only spoken to them once. I given the matter to the LORD; it's in His hands.

I've started the morning in Prayer, ended the night and year in Prayer, and will continue the day in Prayer and Fasting. Time allotted for Social Media has ended for the morning; I've tweeted Jakes, Hinn, Hagee, Wiley, Chirona, and a few others. Look at a few videos of Brister, and an installation of Debra Morton as Prophetess Morton; it's been a good day overall.

It was about 12 noon when I had lunch, then I would fast for the next 7 days as the LORD gives me strength to do so. Later on I watched a little Mike Mille, then my Pastor Owen McManus; both were reruns, and I wondered why. As I write this, a Mocking Bird sits in a tree outside the window. I guess he stopped by to say Hello as the day said goodbye. I'm reading Psalms Chapters 1-9, and it's been a good day.

January 2, 2015 … Friday

I woke to the same thing I fell asleep to. As I sat in my car, I was enjoying the quietness in my car as I sat in the

12 Months From NOW

driveway of my Brother's place, and I must have dozed off. I text a friend; got no response, and I guess that's best. The only thing she has going for her is her thinness, tallness, and her gender; other than that, no compatibility. I don't drink, smoke, or get high and she does; a pointless attraction with no chance of becoming more. After our break-up, my ex used to say that I thought I was better than some. But I didn't think I was better, I just knew the reality of Life says that there are different types of people in the world. Some like the "dirty & gritty" side of Life; I don't. And I don't care to be married or intimate with that facet of life ; so that ends that phone encounter.

I was going to Fast for the next 7 days, but my head is already aching, and my legs and arms are cramping. BP just being difficult; higher than a kite and don't want to cooperate…no matter how I pray. I've changed my diet, even lost a few pounds once, but still no change. Sometimes I just don't know why some conditions in the body are so stubborn to change. I will keep praying though. When it is a miracle you need, your only option is to wait on GOD;…so wait I do.

January 4, 2015… Sunday night…11pm

Today was an interesting day; I was stuck on the westbank due to very little fuel in my gas tank, so I didn't get to my church today. I also haven't heard from the committee on whether I would be allowed to host the event I felt lead to do. It's already been about 5 weeks since I turned in the application.

So even though I didn't get to my church, I was invited to a friend's church; and long with that invite, I still got to go to three (3) churches today.

The friend's church I was invited to was a great disappointment; I walked out after about 20 minutes. It was too much "BS" for a church service. It was my first time there, and the guest speaker was some professor from a Seminary; he was talking incredibly about nothing. I called my friend and told her I had to leave. If it is the "House of the LORD, let me at least hear something that pertains to GOD, instead of self and all their accomplishments. I tried to stay, but it really was too much to bear.

As I left that church and headed to another, I made a quick stop that was not planned. This too was a church service, but it was being held in a school auditorium. I had heard about this particular Pastor holding service in this school, and as I passed the building, I was lead to stop and see for myself. By the time I left I was amazed at what I had just witness. If I was a novice, or new to Ministry work I probably would have missed it. But by now, I can tell a money game when I see one. I could not believe hat I was seeing. To the average person it would look like an ordinary church service. But the truth of the rumors and stories about this Ministry had already been confirmed to me more than once.

Now I was seeing it with my own eyes. Imagine if you saw a 3 yr old child alone on the street at 3a.m.; you would think, "Something is wrong with this picture." This is what I thought when I saw this Pastor finally arrive, standing in the so-called pulpit conducting service with dark shades on. You just don't wear dark shades in church; unless you have something to hide. And the few minutes I remained as I watched him get the crowd hyped, he never took them off. This scene, coupled with the information I had heard about this man, was very disturbing. If I ever wondered what "wolves in sheep clothing" look like, this person was it. I thought I was amazed when I heard about some of the "life at home" stories, and how he hates (with a passion) this other well known bishop. But to see him in these surroundings, having heard that he has tons of money that he has amassed over the years from his members and a few unsavory sources, I was truly amazed and numb as I left the building.

A few minutes later, I arrived at the 3rd church of the day. I sat in my usual seat toward the rear. Nothing extraordinary occurred; but then I haven't seen anything extraordinary happen in church in quite a while. The only time I've witness "tongues" and the "interpretation of tongues" in a church was while I was at "White Dove". And that was many years ago. And the "Word of Knowledge" gift was only witness at "Glory of Christ Christian Center" where I started out as a Youth Pastor. And you know that's been over 20 years ago. A typical church service today begins at a set time, ends at a set time, and everything in between has been rehearsed and planned. So what room is there for the Holy Spirit to show up & show out?…absolutely no room.

Churches today are either boring, or entertaining. And just like the words & meaning of the Bible was kept from the people by the "church"; the HOLY SPIRIT is being kept from the people by the church today.

As I was praying the other day, I thought about something the LORD spoke to me many years ago. HE said,

"You take care of my House, and I'll take care of yours."

As I think about this promise, I can remember thinking it was for the time that it was spoken more 15 years ago. But now I realized that maybe it wasn't just for

then. Maybe it encompassed the NOW, and the days that lies ahead as well.

I said a special Prayer, and turned in for the night; as I wait for the manifestation of all the Prayers I've prayed every day of my life.

January 5, 2015..Monday morning

Today the LORD awaken me at 3:36 a.m. (the 3'oclock hour) like HE normally does. Of course I knew there would be a lesson I would be getting. I soon learned that the Teacher of the day was one of my favorites "Dr. Lester Summeral", a great Man of GOD…and of course the lesson was powerful.

He talked about Prophecies; the titles that many in churches wear out of vanity; and understanding the Word of GOD without taking from or adding to. He reiterated that the WORD is anointed and consecrated, and not to be handled lightly.

I love when the LORD nudges me awake; it's been going on for over 20 years now, and it's always the 3 o'clock hour. I've heard this hour mentioned by a few other Men of Old that I've studied, and there has to be something to this time of the hour.

When I am awaken, I already know that there is something the LORD wants me to do, to learn, or to Pray about. The experience is always an eye-opener on a subject, a confirmation of something HE has already shown me, or taught. It grieves me when I think about the many leaders in church that lend on men for guidance, when the HOLY SPIRIT is right there to help. That's why HE was sent, and that's why we always say, "something told me";… It's the HOLY SPIRIT guiding us. Because HE is the only one here on earth with us; GOD the Father and JESUS is in Heaven.

So much of what is supposed to be Ministry today, is actually a watered down version. A" form of godliness that denies the power thereof; so that's why much that happens in churches today is lukewarm. Maybe I'll send an invitation to all the churches in the city, an invite them to a HOLY GHOST service. Where nothing is planned;…other than Prayer & fasting. No guest speaker other than the HOLY

SPIRIT. No pre planned music;…just selections as the Spirit leads.

I know…sounds weird compared to today's way of having church service.

January 7, 2015…8:33pm…Wednesday

I just left church; it was the first Wednesday Bible study of the New Year. Associate Pastor Jonathan preached. I learned that he has been with the church for 23 years; he's 28. I guess one can say that he's Pastor's "grown son" since he has literally been raised under his wings. Overall, the service was ok; they didn't have "belong night" though, and I was surprised. A corporate Fast from the 5th to the 25 of January has been mandated by

Pastor. I think its "no meat" Fast, but I'm really not sure. I haven't been to service in 2 or 3 weeks thanks to my crazy life. But that's my fault; I'm the one who said when I was young "I didn't want a normal life"…and it's been far from normal. Well as for the corporate fast, I'll try to get more info on it. I make it a point to Fast almost every Sunday because I recognize the importance of it. This and Prayer are basic principles that everyone in Ministry should embraced and implement in their daily lives.

I received a call from Justin, and he apologize for not getting back with me. He said the Board didn't meet last month due to the holidays, so that was the reason for the delay. With the delay, of course I had to change the proposed date of the event from January to February or March. And in spite of my tendency to flourish when the atmosphere is filled with spontaneity, I knew I needed to move the date because a week of preparation for the event would be cutting it too close. But in spite of all the planning, deep down inside I just didn't believe it would happen. I'm considered an "outsider" by church standards. And knowing church people like I do, they don't look to kindly to people just coming into the church trying to implement new ideas. Even if they do come from the Holy Spirit, based on the Word of GOD, and objective is to win Souls for the Kingdom.

As I struggle with these plans, I'm still waiting on a financial blessing from GOD to just get me from one day to the next. I say "from GOD" because in spite of the millions of Millionaires that exist, the many churches that collect millions every Sunday, and the numerous charitable organizations that give away money...none of them give a hoot about what GOD has called me to do. Everybody has their own agenda, and I have to respect that; so I turn to the LORD for help...that's my only option.

My African friend is still trying to get me to move back to Texas; I keep telling him it is out of the question; at least out of the question on a full-time basis. I have a house in mind that I want to buy located in Arlington. It's very contemporary, and I love it. This a house I was looking to buy before the ex went off the deep end. It was listed at about $470 thousand, and with the houses & apartments I owned, along with my job, I could have easily afforded it. But that dream died with a few others three (3) years ago. But I gotta keep "moving & dreaming"…GOD is still in control.

I didn't do anything for Christmas or New Years; just gotta keep praying for a change. Don't know when, but hopefully soon. I'm sooo tired of being broke, and full of so many dreams & ideas; its sooo very frustrating. I found a letter from Marilyn Hickey with a packet of anointing oil in it. Prayed, anointed myself from head to toe, and now I'll just WAIT….but then what choice do I have?

January 8, 2015…Thursday

I awaken about 6a.m.; didn't actually get up till about 6:45. The rest of the house wasn't up till about 9a.m.; I'm over by my

Sister at the moment; the one that is close by my church. She likes me to spent lots of time over here at her house; it works out of when I need to get to church with very little gas in my car. I haven't worked a real job in 2 years, but that's another story.

Went to the library to finish doing my Son's taxes; I got back at about 7pm. Also spoke with Jennifer about coming down to her place in Ponchatoula to edit & publish her book. We talked for about an hour, and she is very excited about the whole thing. She says she has been waiting for 6 years to get her book done. I also talked with a guy over at TBN media dept. Learned that it cost from $2000 to $14000 per episode to have a program aired on TBN. And then you have to commit to a 52 week deal. So that's $2000 to $14000 dollars times 52;

that comes to a lot of money. Prayed; gave the matter to GOD, and moved on to the next idea.

January 9, 2015…Friday

The day started at 6:30a.m. even though I didn't lay down till after 2:00a.m. I was up watching "12 year Slave"; it was hard at first but I made it through. For some reason I felt I needed to watch it; so I did. I was surprised to learn that it was directed by Steve McQueen.By 10a.m. I had taken my Sister to her Doctor appt; and stopped by my friend since I was in the area. Her name is Eunice, and she's a Realtor/Broker; we chatted for a few minutes then I left because she is always very busy. I picked up a magazine while there, and at the time I didn't know it. But this magazine was what got me to start an internet Radio show. And I learned later that it was hosted by the daughter of a well

known local News Celebrity. The show is called "LetsLive Radio.com" and it was indeed a leading of Holy Spirit.

I normally listen to CeCe's Throne Room CD but I'm chillin with a little EWF. Growing up, these guys were the most during my teenage years. I can go on & on, but I won't. Even my kids know how their Daddy feels about Earth, Wind, & Fire. Thank You LORD…it's been a Good Day.

12 Months From NOW

January 10, 2015…Saturday

I dropped my sister off at her church for practice; then I met with a guy who was selling a townhouse duplex for $99,000 dollars. His name was Stan and he was a very nice guy. We talked for a least 2 hours, and I really did like the property, but wasn't that crazy about the location. After I left, I said a prayer and asked the LORD to send him a buyer since it had been listed for a while; and it didn't matter if I was the buyer, or someone else. As long as he got his wish; and got his duplex sold. It may seem strange to some but I talk to GOD all through the day, and I'm sure I send up at least 10-20 prayers a day for various circumstances. If you are a true Christian, Praying should be as frequent as

eating, drinking, and going to the potty….I'm just saying.

January 19, 2015…Monday morning

Didn't make it to church; no gas in the car and no money in my life at the moment. I've been missing my kids a lot; the little ones and the adult ones. Even had a dream about finding/getting a place soon because my girls will be with me soon. So I guess I'll Pray little harder for provisions to be met;…Amen.

(2 months later)

March 25, 2015...Wednesday, Bible Study

If you notice, the last entry took place on the 19th of January 2015. It is now March 25, 2015. I just left City Church 7:00 p.m. Bible study. This is my first day back, after being gone since the last week of January 2015.

Service was great. Mike Babylon preached; he was one of the elders. Prior to this of course, I didn't know his name. But like most in the church, I just know faces. He titled his message the Lord gave him "CHRIST is enough". I sat there feeling like a stranger after being gone so long. But I didn't feel this way because I lacked time with GOD, this feeling came from a few things that happen the last time I was in attendance. But I just ignored them, because I knew that my being there has nothing to do with me. This is where I was sent, and so this is where I AM.

I wanted to stay and attend a "Growth group" but I've already attended a few in my attempt to fit in; it just isn't working. I was thinking about it as I was leaving, and this thought came to mind. The LORD by HIS HOLY SPIRIT is the only one that can take credit for what I've been taught. He used men, Women, children, situations, Friends, Family, Strangers, and Churches. As well as Pastors, Elders, Members, of the churches, and the WORD. And even though many in attendance at City Church may have a need for the "Growth classes", I'm not one of them. I'm not a babe in Christ, and I haven't just recently got introduced to church life. Unlike some that are in leadership roles, I know when the Bible is being misquoted. I'll never forget a quote one of the elders made while teaching a class that I chose to sit in on. She said,

"…Faith comes BEFORE hearing the Word…".

I just shook my head, thinking, "and you gonna teach me…yea right."

Then when I raised my hand later to share the experience I just had in the parking lot earlier, they looked at me and just ignored me. Like I was not qualified to speak, interject a comment, or even be acknowledged. Maybe I was breaking some cardinal rule; but I thought it very rude to be ignored so blatantly. I felt like I was a high school graduated being asked to attend kindergarten again, just because I was one of the "new members" and I wasn't familiar with their way of doing things.

I felt whatever role I'm to be used in by GOD, while I'm at City Church, that role will compliment whatever he has give the Pastor. It will not disrupt, clash, nor take away from the "Vision" already in place.

Over the years, I've seen the territorial spirit that many churches possess. Even though it says, and they say its "the House of GOD" they act like it's their personal property. Folks are constantly on guard, think everybody that say they were sent, was "sent by satan". So for this reason, the Spirit of the LORD can't even ENTER in

GOD's house. Because other "Spirits" have taken over.

The Lord tells us to "test the spirits"; so as Christians we need to test them; and stop being so carnal & fleshly. HE has given many "gifts" to the Body of Christ, yet we use so few of them.

…Gift of Discernment;

Gift of prophecy,

Gift of Word of Knowledge,

Gift of Healing,

Gift of Tongues,

And Gift of Interpretation of Tongues.

Yes the LORD has given us many Gifts, to be used as we go through life. With these gifts, we don't need to be fearful, suspicious, or intimidated. Over the years,

I have been taught how to TRUST HIM, and HE wants the Body of Christ to learn how to TRUST HIM. The Churches today do not TRUST GOD; and the sad part is that they think they do.

I left church, and went home. Not because I wanted to; but because I didn't want to "go to kindergarten" again.

Now 20 years ago, I was pretty "green" when it came to ministry. If you said you were a Pastor or Reverend, I believed anything you said. But the LORD needed me to learn a very important lesson real quick. And that lesson was,

"that there are many wolves in sheep clothing."

And I needed to KNOW the difference.

That lesson cost me over $200,000 plus dollars, several houses, many cars, and lots of opportunities. And not to mention the time that was lost. But I learned the lesson, and have there forgotten the "wolves" aspect of ministry.

I walked to the opposite side of the sanctuary after Bible study was over. It was only my 2nd time in 2 years, but I wanted to say Hi and talked to Pastor Benson before I left. I did it only because he did a friend request on one of my FB accounts about 3 weeks earlier. I didn't see a point of being FB friends on the internet, and not be acquaintance in real life. I would consider that a bit hypocritical; especially for church folks.

But I know what prompt the request. In November I submitted a request to the church to rent the building to host an event. Of course its Ministry related. But

12 Months From NOW

I'm an unknown, so the sense of caution is evident. And due to the busy schedule (I want to believe is the reason) I didn't get a denial until 3 months later. Afterwards, I requested a reason in writing. I felt that sense I submitted the application in writing, it was only proper for a decision to be made in writing as well. Of course I didn't want to seem difficult; but afterwards it seems like folks were passing me and not saying Hi. So I just ignored the rudeness and just blew it off. And later told myself, "we're all still learning."

So after the denial, I called and requested a meeting with the Pastor. The person that answered was very rude. I've been in business and dealing with all types of people all my life, and I know when I'm being handled badly on the phone. As if I've been black-balled. Ignoring the rudeness, I again told myself, "we're all just learning."

Now, I'm only mentioning these incidents so those that might be reading about them may learn something from them. Our job in Ministry is to build one another up, and learn from our mistakes. Because we're all going to make them. The key is to not ignore them, but go to our brother if we have offended them…and clear the air. Apologize, make amends, do what is necessary and be sincere about it. Then we can go to GOD, and HE will hear our prayers.

During tonight's service, the same person that saw me months earlier, walked within 2 feet of me and you could tell they were acting as if I was invisible. I don't know at what point I may have offended them by something I said or done, but I'll be sure to get with them and find out…and soon. I'll be sure to pray beforehand because I don't want satan drama on my part, or theirs.

Well my chat with Dr. Benson was only for about a minute. After 20 years of dealing with churches & church people, I'm purposely a bit stand-offish now. Over the years I've notice that people sometimes assume your friendliness as a means of trying to get close with the Pastor. And that's never been something I've needed. I know GOD; and HE knows me. My relationship to the Pastor is only going to be in direct relationship to the job GOD has called me to do. And in the course of trying to complete the assignment at City Church, (and it is an assignment) GOD has had me to be in communication with two other Pastors. I met one two weeks ago while on another assignment. This assignment involved Publishing a Book for a client; a first time author.

As of March 22, 2015 that mission is accomplished, and the client is ecstatic with satisfaction. I prayed before I left, gave GOD the thanks & glory, and now I'm back here home in New Orleans. And this is how I arrived back at my church, after being gone for several months. I've been working on several titles for the past two months. It was a lot of work, but thank GOD the job (an assignment) is completed and I'm so very thankful.

The books have been on Amazon.com now for less than a week. Now comes the "PR campaign". The client Jennifer "jupie" Thompson's book is called the "The Outhouse." It's a very great story, and she and her family is so happy with how it all turned out. I'm considering also writing the screenplay since I was also the Managing Editor on the project. Not to mention designing the cover, writing the Cover outline, and being the photographer as well.

During this rather busy 2 months, I also published 3 of my own books and designed the Covers, wrote the outline for all, and take credit for all the Cover Photos. Yes…it's been a very busy two months. My three (3) titles are: "The GHOST in the FOURTH Bedroom", "12 Months from Now Book I", and "Just Another Messenger of GOD." I'm working on getting three (3) more out by this weekend. There titles are "Names of Demonic & Evil Spirits" ,"12 Months From Now Book II", 12 Months from

Now Book III", and the H-bomb of them all …"Bastards & Bitches." All tools to Preach the Gospel of JESUS CHRIST to a dying and Lost Generation.

If you have been called to reach them, you have to speak the language they understand… Street. Then make sure its sprinkled with a lot of Holy Ghost Spirit… because them Demons/Evil Spirits ain't giving up without a fight.

Well before I end this entry, I want to just give a little updated to the current date.

After receiving the denial (which I had been waiting weeks for) to Host the event, I was given an opportunity to Publish a new Author's book. I Prayed about it, waited for the approval from GOD, and then took on the assignment. This has been the reason for my absence from church. And it would also explain my postponing the meeting I requested back then. Prior to this assignment, I was also sent to Minister & meet with another Pastor one Sunday I wasn't able to get to City Church. I met with them; Prayed with them, and the LORD showed me a little of what he wanted to do in this House. The Pastor knew of me, and so did his wife; which attended the same High school as I. And they were very receptive and in agreement in the beginning; when I prayed with them both, they knew it was on point with what GOD was saying. But then I watched his apprehension rise, and soon his wife followed. I even caught her one time secretly recording me with her camera phone while I sat in the back of the church as her husband preached. I acted as if I never noticed it, but I understood her concern though. It occurred only once, and by then I had visit with them at least 10 times, going to their service after leaving City Church's first service. Now if I was lead to remain at City Church, I did. I even attended a few of their Bible studies on Tuesday. By then, they were very nervous of me and "my agenda." I knew GOD just wanted to come in the House, and show them how to TRUST him more. Then after promising to take me out to lunch at least 3 or 4 times (it never materialize). One day while at home the Holy Spirit told me,

"He is reluctant to call you because you are an enigma to him."

I later shared this with them (and the very few members in attendance) one night. But he still didn't do anything about it. So soon I was given another assignment, and head to Pontchatoula, LA.

Never been there before, but it was a very nice two month stay, while working on several manuscripts. I didn't attend any churches while out there, because I just didn't know any in the area; plus I was very busy. The book was almost 400 pages, and because the manner in which it was written (no proper punctuations), it took me about 20 minutes for every 2 pages. So in between sleeping, it was quite a job. The client was also a family friend, so I was invited to "crash" till I completed the assignment. So when I completed it, I cleaned the room, got on my knees and thank the LORD for his assistance and then departed; heading back to New Orleans.

It is now 1a.m.; I left church about 7:45p.m. Five (5) hours ago. When I got here at my Sister who lives about 1 ½ mile from City Church, I was starving. But I knew I need to get started on Book IV, and having learned over the years the power of fasting, I postponed the eating till I get some work done; and get some words on paper. I've also been listening to CeCe Winans "Throne Room" (my favorite of her work) with headphones... sounds so wonderful! I have also learned the value of anointed music when I'm working. And from CeCe, we went to 2 hours of Fred Hammond LIVE. Then Israel Houghton "LIVE in South Africa. When I finish this entry, I'm going go and bless my food, and eat. I had one meal today ;2 chicken wing drumettes... bout 2" and a lil Tampico orange juice. Early today I walked about 2 miles (need to stay in shape) took a few photographs on the lake of the horizon, and met a guy named Max from Palestine operating a corner store. When I told him my name, he insisted that I was not from New Orleans…I didn't argue. When he insisted on knowing where I was from and what was my heritage, I said French. Which may be true since part my name is French (Finis). It means the End…no kidding. And yes, these are the Last Days, my name means Last or the end, and GOD called me to Preach in these Last Days. I call it GOD's sense of humor when I realized all this.

He then shook my hand, and said he was very glad to meet me; I reciprocated the response.

As I bring this entry to a closed, Israel song "I have not forgotten…He knows my name" is playing thru the headphone..

..I'm Jammin! But that's what I do when it comes to the Gospel of JESUS CHRIST!

…until we read again.

1:31a.m… Page 31

Sunday, March 30, 2015

Well…I waited all week for this day, and now it has finally come. Three churches later, and I'm still looking & hoping to experience the power of GOD in these supposedly "Houses of GOD".

The Sunday started off with me dropping my sister off at her church for 8a.m. My church didn't start until 9a.m. so I headed back to the house to study the Word, work a bit on the manuscripts, an continue to watch a view more Youtubes videos on Charles Spurgeon. He was another church pioneer that made an impact on Ministry in the early part of the 1900's. I had finished up with a few studies on William Tyndale, and I found his life to be very interesting. He was reformer of the mid 1500's who defied the rules and practices of the Roman Catholic Church. He was fluent in German, Greek, Italian, Hebrew, Portuguese, and his native English, and was burned at the stake for translating the Bible to English. And the Roman Catholic Church was the executioner; back then people were not allowed to know what the Bible said. William Tyndale played a very vital role in the King James Bible that we are privileged to read to day. And because I know it cost the blood of men, this is the only version I trust to read. For it is the one I know has been ordained by GOD; for it came with a price.

By 8: 45a.m. I was ready to head to my church, and arrived with about 10 minutes to spare. Greeted the usual Greeters, and headed to my usual seat. The right side of the sanctuary, 2nd section, seat on the end. I kneel and said a prayer (first time), and got ready for whatever was to come.

Music was "bumpin" and the light show was entertaining, and as usual the young crowd was enjoying it all. It was a typical Sunday service here at my church. By the third song, I stood also to join in the singing. "Your Name is JESUS" was being song, and it had more of an anointing on it, for which I could relate.

Pastor's wife joined the rest on the stage, said a few Announcements, and directed our attention to the week's additional Announcements.

The 2nd annual (I think it's the 2nd) Easter Egg Drop was mentioned, along with the new Westbank location officially opening for Palm Sunday, and the 3 day Corporate Fast mandated by Pastor, As I sat there, I thought about the first time I heard about all of this. I'm not an expert in the area of church business, but I have 20+ years of experience, and I cannot deny the things that the Spirit of the LORD shows me when it comes to church business.

First of all, the church climate of today believes that they have to go where the people are…I don't agree. That is totally contrary to Bible. People will come, where the Spirit of the Lord is; no need to advertise, go where they are, or use "growth tactics" to get seats filled. And being that I visited 3 churches today, I saw this practiced being preached in one church, and implemented in another, and I find it very disturbing.

And as for as the Easter event, when I heard of it a week earlier I thought ,

" I don't get it." This is what I've seen over the years when it comes to church activities. More time and energy is spent on getting the people in the church, than time spent on getting the "Presence of GOD" in the church. Now we all have heard it said every Sunday, in every church, about the "presence of GOD" being in church with us. But if the "presence of GOD was really in churches like we say HE is… U would know it,

U would see it,

U would feel it,

And believe it.

And News crews would be out front before the day was over. Because Sickness cannot remain in the "presence o f GOD"; neither can disease, deformities, or demons & evil spirits. In the Presence, there will be Healings & Deliverances all over the place. And people would be coming from miles around to get a taste of "GOD's presence."   And the Brownsville Revival of 1995 wasn't even close to the "Move & Presence of Almighty GOD. When man truly get out of the way, and stop trying to lay claim to things of GOD by trying to share in HIS GLORY with their "religious tags" and carnal ideas, they will really began to see a true "Move of GOD."

GOD has wanted to do this upon the whole earth, but Man just refuse to get out of the way, or let go of their religious ideas & practices. So the Revival that all the church people are talking about and wanting, is being held up by the same group of people that are praying for it. I was shown this by the Holy Spirit more than 15 years ago.

More preparations must be made to usher in the Holy Spirit, and that is just not happening. Churches think they are worshipping GOD with their music, but it's just noise. It sounds good to us, but it's just noise to GOD.

If one really study the different varieties of musical instruments, you will learn that they are governed by different spirits. This is noted in the Book of I Samuel 16:14-23 when David was called to play a particular instrument for Saul to get the Evil Spirit to depart from him. And when you put together the right types of instruments for worship, you will get the right type of sound, to usher in the right kind of atmosphere. And the right musical atmosphere, with the right Prayer atmosphere, and everyone on one accord, in a consecrated place, will produce the perfect atmosphere to usher in the "Presence of GOD".

But in today's churches, just like anyone is used to Pray for others, anyone is used to worship and attempt to usher in the Holy Spirit. No one has fasted, probably no one has prayed, and if the place is not a consecrated place, the Holy Spirit will not be showing up. Over the years I've seen people open up churches just anywhere. Store-fronts, homes, multipurpose buildings, their garage, even schools, and hotel banquet rooms. No consecration whatsoever, and I just…smh.

Pastor went on to preach a message about tithing, and it was very interesting. I made sure I put my $2 tithe in. Even though I have several books published on Amazon.com, and did it only through Prayer & Fasting every day, I haven't had a real income in two years. After the ex-wives LIE, no one is hiring me. Being falsely charged with a sexual crime will cause quite a bit of damage. But again, that's another story.

So back to the subject of tithing; I know it's another subject I feel the LORD has me dealing with. The Book was started several weeks ago and it is called, "Why Do the Preachers Continue to LIE on Malachi". The title came to me about a month ago while I was editing my other titles, and getting them ready to be published by my publishing company named in honor of my mother. It is called TOOSWEETPUBLISHING productions. They are the four books I currently have on Amazon.com. The tithing one is going be quite a doozy because this is a touchy subject with most Christians & church people. Ummm…that's another title for a book : "Are You a Church Person or Christian"… I got to remember that one.

Well after the 9a.m. service, I headed to the westbank. This is my routine when I have gas in my vehicle, and I'm lead to make a visit. It's been months since I have visit with this church as well, and I'm sure they've wonder where I've been. Well it would be best if they did, because they must remember; this too was not my idea. GOD lead me to this church just like HE lead me to my own. And just like my own, HE has plan for this Church. But if they don't take me serious, well the backlash is going to be on them. Because GOD does everything for a reason, and even when you are involved in something GOD is doing, and you don't even have a clue why YOU are involved, its best to just stay Pray Up, in the Word, and Fasting on a regular basis. Because by doing so, you'll less likely be wrong about your personal involvement. For if you ask GOD for direction, do you honestly think HE would steer you wrong?...NOT ever!

Well arrived to this church at about 5 minutes till 11:00a.m.; service would have stared at 10:a.m. As I crossed the street and approached the entrance to the sanctuary, I heard the music reverberating from the inside. The seats were 75% full; I was pleasantly surprised. The last time I attended there were less than 20 people in attendance.

I found my normal spot in the back seat on the last row, and simply observed. There was a guest in the front; it wasn't long before I discern it was more of an entertainment atmosphere than an anointed one. And ironically he was singing a song saying, "…it was the anointing." Well by the 5th, 6th, or 7th song (I lost count), I was sure there was no anointing involved in what I was witnessing. Here was a man I didn't know, never heard of, and had never seen before getting the congregation "hyped-up"; and many were really enjoying themselves. I noticed the Pastor and wife were not in their normal spot. I noticed First Lady was sitting in the rear of the church on the other side of the room from where I was sitting, and the Pastor had came from the back and was now sitting with the audio guy near the equipment. I found out later that the guest was enjoying a repeat performance from the previous Sunday. I don't know if it was his first or second one, but he was very comfortable with the congregation. And it seem like the "Heads" were very comfortable with him leading the Service. The amazing part about this as I watched it was the fact that I had just watch a video earlier about a message preached cy Charles Spurgeon. In it he talked about the Church and their tendency to "entertain" people. That message was almost a 100 years old, and yet the message was right on point.

We as Christians will never get the Holy Spirit to join us in any church service as long as we are controlling the service. There is no reverence for GOD's House when people walk in; there is no appropriate music to set the atmosphere, and because people have come to believe it's a great time to "catch-up" on the latest, we miss every opportunity for the Holy Spirit to show up & show out.

Well by the time I left, I was even more disappointed by the "taking over of the temple" by the money changers that I was witnessing. Tables & chairs were set up in the sanctuary for people to sit down and eat the food they were now selling in the rear of the church. I won't comment on the discernment I gathered from the "young merchants" that were hocking their wares, but it left me concern. I sense a greater interest in the nutritional value of the food they were selling, and making a sale, than whether anyone would make it to Heaven. It was a very sad image from my perspective, but what can I do, I'm just a visitor. It didn't matter that I was sent here by GOD, or that he personally called me, and specifically sent me home to New Orleans. I discerned early on that if a church was going to have an impact on the City of New Orleans, in some form or fashion, I too would be involved with that church…no matter how big or small the involvement. Now here I was being directly involved with two very distinctly different churches, and learning a wealth of information from both of them. They both should be learning as well, but at the moment, I'm a "nobody" to them both; yet a very distinct "somebody" to GOD.

I said my goodbye to Pastor, truly grieved by what I see he has allowed in GOD's house. But again, I'm just a visitor with only authority from GOD; and if he is not willing to "hear from GOD" from HIS appointed Messenger, then I'm force to witness the not to pleasant end result. Many in the Ministry have good intentions, but I learned early in my training about the "Road to Hell" being paved with a lot of "good intentions". When it comes to the "things of GOD", good intentions are of very little use.

The thing that is guaranteed to work are: PRAYER,

FASTING,

Reading the WORD,

More PRAYER & FASTING,

And more WORD. And finally,

12 Months From NOW

"to always expect the unexpected". Because GOD hardly every do what we expect. JESUS birth is a prime example.

Outside of this approach, there is very little chance of getting anything done for GOD. For HE clearly says,

"His ways are not our ways; and His thoughts are not our thoughts".

I left the westbank, stopped and had my usual Popeye's Breast that I buy maybe once a month, and then headed back to East New Orleans. I thought about my dream place as I neared the G.N.O. but I opt not to pass over there this day. I haven't seen it in over 3 months as well, but I'm still praying for a break-thru to purchase it for cash, have it given to me, or any other means; as long as I get possession of it as Owner.

I would have written when I made it to my sister's place, but I was too tired; so I took a nap. By the time I awaken, it was close to taking my sister to her church for the 2nd time. But this time I stayed an enjoyed the "Women's day" program. First Lady preached, and it was good seeing her. She asked about the books I published, and we chatted a bit about them. Overall, the program was nice; my Sister enjoys her dance group "Anointed 2Praise". The day ended with my 3 unplanned Church visits; and it was interesting day overall. What I got out of the day overall is that the majority of churches do not have the HOLY SPIRIT even though they say that they do. And they don't have it because preparations have not really been made for HIS Presence. It's more about keeping the people's attention; but if the majority really knew GOD, the biggest problem would be getting them to go Home.

I don't know what to expect come Wednesday, but I'll see when I get there. I'm not sure what date this volume is schedule to end, but I'll just stay tuned as the HOLY SPIRIT leads. This "church business" was HIS idea anyway. BE BLESS people of GOD!

Sunday Morning…Easter Sunday, 2015

As I come to the End of this page, I also come to the end of this Book series. Whether it has accomplished what GOD intended, only GOD knows. I felt lead to write it, so I did.

Now I had no clue when It would end, but it being the close of Easter Sunday I find it to be symbolic. Jesus rose on the 3rd Day which was the start of his Heavenly Ministry as the Resurrected CHRIST…a New Beginning.

As I rose from my 4 a.m. Prayer this Monday morning, I thought about all that I'd seen, heard, and been through as a Man of GOD. Loved by his children; rejected by his wives; adored by Friends & Family, and Forgiven by CHRIST, I asked GOD for a New Beginning. Whatever I lacked in this first part of my journey, I be given; whatever I possess or have that I don't need, it be taken from me; and whatever I overlooked, that HE would take care.

In this journey I have seen that "The Church" today have become more of a building than a People that love & obey

GOD. The Music in the Church reflect the World, the Message reflects the World, and the People also reflect the World. Everyone wants to be different, stand-out, unique. Yet GOD has already made us different, unique, stand out & set apart. So we don't have to color our hair purple, blue, and red. Pierce, tattoo, and alter our bodies. Chop off our own hair, and add the dead hair of others. Are we that dissatisfied with ourselves (and GOD) and confused that we actually think that we can improve on the work of GOD? Are we serious?

The Bible says that "all good things come from GOD"; yet if you look around at the state of the world, society as a whole, and people, you will notice that there quite a few things that are not so good. Killing & murder is like a past-time for some; satan has even fooled this generation into making it a game, and thinking it is ok. Theft and robbery is as common as the sand on the seashore. Lying has become a deceptive, but respected profession. Adultery, fornication, & whoredom is big business, and no longer frown upon. And Perversion is no longer just a thing of the past; it is an accepted practice by law.

Easter Sunday being a big day for church-goers, I opt not to attend. Now some would be aghast at such a practice, when the Bible caution us, "…as the manner of some is..". But isn't one's motive for going to church more important than the fact that you are going? Why else would GOD say "depart from me ye workers of iniquity; I never knew you". He was talking to the people "in the world", but people "in the church".

12 Months From NOW

Wherever we find ourselves in Life, we all must know GOD for ourselves. And no matter who we are, where we are from, how much money we possess, or how many degrees, gifts, or talents we have…we CAN NOT impress GOD with them. Ever knee will bow, and every tongue will confess…that HE (JESUS) is LORD. A building will not save Us; neither will a religion. Only a RELATIONSHIP with the FAHER, that comes only through a RELATIONSHIP with the SON…JESUS the CHRIST. The Messiah, and Light of the World.

So if you found yourself to be one of those who ran to the pretty building on Easter Sunday, but you really don't know the LORD, say this Prayer:

I'M A SINNER, AND I DON'T KNOW YOU; BUT WANT TO. REVEAL

YOURSELF TO ME, THAT I MAY KNOW YOU. WHATEVER IS IN ME OR A PART OF ME THAT IS NOT OF YOU, OR THAT YOU FIND DISPLEASING, PLEASE TAKE IT OUT & FROM ME. REPLACE IT WITH YOUR SPIRIT LORD JESUS. BY THE WORDS OF MY LIPS, I CONFESS YOU LORD OF MY LIFE; COME INTO MY HEART, AND REMAIN…in your precious name LORD JESUS I pray this Prayer, Amen, Amen, & Amen.

1. Say the" Lord's Prayer" everyday (Go to internet; find Lord's Prayer)
2. Find a Church Home (Pray & ask GOD to choose)
3. Study & Read the Word (the Bible) often. (King James Version)
4. Separate yourself from friends & people who are bad influence

5. Respect yourself & others (especially your Body); no sex if unmarried, don't be a drunkard or overeater)
6. Don't give in to Temptation
7. Be mindful of the music you listen to and things you watch on TV
8. Abstain from Evil, Profanity, & Occult activities
9. Love & Respect GOD; show Love to all (no matter the culture)
10. Enjoy the Life GOD has given YOU

Years ago when I was praying once, the Holy Spirit asked me a question. He said,

"Do You know why we have to ask the LORD to come into our lives?

Because of the lifestyles in which we have lived, have driven HIM out."

And as I think about this now, I just now realize that HE was also telling me that we are born with the "Spirit of GOD" in us. Look at the face, and in the eyes of a child, a Baby…how can you not see the Spirit of GOD in them.

But then we grow-up, learn how to Lie, steal, cheat, and love the things of this world, and hate the things of GOD. And this is why we have to ask JESUS back into our Hearts.

As I close, I leave with you an article I wrote (never published) after watching a PBS program. I ran across it as I was preparing to finish this book series. I Believe it speaks for itself, and is a perfect analogy to what has happen to us as Church people (CHRISTIANS) and people in the world.

"JEWS IN HISTORY... Is it a culture, religion, or status symbol?"

By SIR...theSOULman

I just finish watching a program on PBS showcasing the history of Jews & the Jewish culture here in New Orleans. It mentioned the many Jewish family names that have been a part of New Orleans history for generations. Like the names Touro, Delgado, Godcheaux, Woldenburg, and a host of others. As I watched the program, and thought about the history of the "children of Israel," I founded it amazing how things tend to evolve over time...and not so much for the better.

As I watched the program, I notice that the Judaism they spoke of had become more of a culture or social concern, instead of a "people's relationship with GOD." And since being called to the Ministry many years ago, studying the word of GOD is not only a requirement for me, but also a pastime. In my study time, I'm often amazed at some of the events that happen to the people during that time, and the similar occurrences of people today. Example...when the people of GOD would arrive in to a new area amongst people of different cultures, beliefs, and traditions, it was always stressed to them, not to become like the people of that region. Not to worship their false gods, not to embrace their pagan religions, and not to marry their people. Well...time & time again the "people of GOD" would forget these instructions, embrace the practices and beliefs of these ungodly people, and push the true & living GOD's laws & instructions in the back of their minds. After watching this PBS program, it seems like the Jewish people of New Orleans has done the same.

And as I look even deeper, I see this happening today amongst the many so called Believers/Christians. So much compromising in their living, their way of worshiping GOD, and even thinking it's ok to join their religious beliefs with the practices & beliefs of pagan thinkers:

"It's ok to Do & Be like the world; GOD's a loving God, he'll forgive us."

"Come on…it's just a tattoo; body art; it's no big deal."

"Why get married; lets live together first; plus it's just a piece of paper anyway."

Yet the Bible says,

"…be ye in the world, but not of the world."

Many must think these words or just some sort of "bumper sticker" slogan, and not words to live by.

From this PBS program of the Jewish people influence in New Orleans history, I saw that there were many different opinions of the Jewish people, and even the Jewish people themselves had various kinds of opinions of one another. It seems there is the "orthodox Jew" that embraced the old way; the "reform Jew" that incorporated new ideas with the old; A the one never even mentioned, was the "Christian Jew" which I learned years earlier, was an oxymoron like the term jumbo-shrimp. It was during my study in the Ministry that I learned that Jews (the chosen people of GOD) was not Christians. I thought to myself,

"How can that be?"

And from the PBS program, it seems that many seem to see their Jewish heritage as a social status symbol, reserved for the rich and influential, instead of a people with a very special relationship with the Almighty GOD of heaven, and earth.

As a teenager, I grew up believing that Jews were very close to GOD. I was astonished when after being called to the Ministry, I learned a very strange and profound truth. Jesus was born in Bethlehem in a manager according to the Bible (which is the inspired Word of GOD), over 2000 years ago. The Jewish people are the chosen people of GOD, and yet it is common knowledge that they are taught that this event has not occurred…and this astounded me!

JESUS (the Messiah) that has been prophesied to them for thousands of years, the same one that they have been waiting for, they believe is yet to be born. And the JESUS that we all know as a Christian is somehow not the Messiah. And from this I thought,

"Wow, if they have allowed themselves to be fooled and believe a LIE, what hope do we have as "biblical Gentiles?"

Then I realized,

"We know the Truth and have the Truth because we have the Holy Spirit."

The Jews that don't believe that JESUS is the Messiah, are blinded because the Word of GOD says,

"The god of this world (satan) has their eyes blinded."

So if they don't believe the "here-now-JESUS" is the true Messiah, then how can they hear or receive anything from the "here-now-Holy Spirit?"

So not allowing the Holy Spirit to influence and lead & guide them, they have become more worldly & carnal. Judaism is seen more as a symbol of social and financial status, instead of a symbol of a chosen religious people of the True and Living GOD.

If we look around today, everything that belongs to GOD has been infiltrated with, and by the things of the world, satan, or man which the Bible says sometimes is one in the same. For example:

1. Church…the building where we suppose to find GOD is reeking with the traditions of men, and sprinkled with a few known & unknown influences of the devil. Idols & objects worshipped throughout these

buildings; activities & practices that don't even reflect godly principles; and chosen locations that have a past that should have never even been considered for a place of GOD's "house of worship."

2. Religion…can't even recognize GOD in most of the religions of today. They are so self-serving and money driven that GOD wouldn't be caught in many of the so-called "religious" places. There is only one True & Living GOD, but thousands of different religions & religious beliefs; somehow throughout time, some got influenced by satan and allowed themselves to form "new ways" to reach GOD. But JESUS says HE is the only WAY, the TRUTH, and the LIGHT…no man

comes to the Father except by HIM. So many if not all the religions of today, simply has it wrong.

3. Marriage…if satan has not infiltrated this holy & blessed example, and Godly representation of a union between a man & a woman by trying to enjoin it to the gay lifestyle,…then "grits & grocery, eggs ain't poultry, and Mona Lisa was a man."

Yes, I'm **SIR…the SOULman**; and I sit back and look at LIFE and wonder how we got to be so far from our original state…so far from where GOD intended us to be. Yet GOD says in the Book of Proverbs,

"Man was made upright/good in the beginning, but he have sought out many inventions."

In other words, mankind has allowed themselves to be influenced by satan, even though they started out with a great advantage being the children of Almighty GOD.

It's not easy, and has not been easy since I was called by GOD to preach the Gospel but,

"I study to show myself approved; a workman that needed not to be ashamed; rightfully dividing the Word of Truth."

So I dare not try to inject my opinion when it comes to speaking or writing on the subject of the "things of GOD," or a perspective; because what I think, feel, or believe is irrelevant. Only what GOD says matters, not the opinions or viewpoint of me, or any man for that matter. In the past, some have considered some of the things I've spoken to be a bit bold, and offensive. But the LORD says,

"…open up your mouth, and I will give you the words to speak."

So a man or woman lead of the Spirit of GOD, may come across as being offensive to some; especially those that may still be living in SIN or,

"walking the path that seemeth right, but whose path leadeth to destruction."

In other words, someone doing their own thing, and whatever pleases them, is not going to ever agree or like what a Prophet of GOD says. Why? Because the Bible says that the Word of GOD is foolishness to those that are perishing.

If that "Man or Woman of GOD" is speaking and operating under the anointing and influence of Almighty GOD, they can't help but speak the TRUTH, and what

"…thus saith the LORD."

An obedient servant of GOD is going to say only what GOD place in their heart, and in their mouths; they are not going to inject their opinions or viewpoints into the matter when they have been instructed by GOD. And a true people of GOD, will shrug the traditions of men, turn back to GOD & the laws & practices of GOD, and remember from whence they come, and the heritage of their forefathers.

If we are TRUE BELIEVERS in CHRIST, we ought to reflect this in everything we say & do…without compromise.

If GOD said it, BELIEVE IT and DO IT!...if HE didn't… DON'T!

...can't get no simpler than that.

I AM, SIR…the SOULman, called of ALMIGHTY GOD to Preach, Teach, LIVE, and Proclaim the Gospel of JESUS CHRIST.
I will do it in season & out of season; come "hell or high water" (like Katrina).

Whether it's received or believed.
As a Messenger & Servant of GOD, it is my job to deliver the message; what the recipient does with it after it is delivered …is on them!

Be bless people of GOD; and REPENT for the kingdom of GOD is at hand.

And you/we ARE the Generation that will see it.
…and we ain't just whistling Dixie; we know what we have been shown & told.

…THE END

12 Months From NOW

www.ingramcontent.com/pod-product-compliance
Lightning Source LLC
Chambersburg PA
CBHW061501040426
42450CB00008B/1443